Introduction

In today's digital age, user-generated content (UGC) has become a powerful force in the realm of marketing and brand engagement. UGC, as the name suggests, refers to any form of content created by consumers rather than by brands themselves. This encompasses a wide range of material, from product reviews and testimonials to social media posts, videos, and even podcasts.

What is UGC and why is it important?

UGC holds immense significance in the current marketing landscape due to its authenticity, credibility, and ability to foster a sense of community. Unlike traditional advertising, which is often perceived as biased and promotional, UGC is viewed as more genuine and unbiased, resonating more deeply with consumers. This authenticity stems from the fact that UGC is created by real people sharing their genuine experiences and opinions.

Moreover, UGC serves as powerful social proof, influencing consumer purchasing decisions. When individuals observe others using and endorsing a particular product or service, they are more likely to develop a positive perception of that offering. This social proof effect is particularly prevalent among millennials and Gen Z consumers, who place a high value on peer recommendations and authentic experiences.

Furthermore, UGC plays a crucial role in building brand communities and fostering a sense of connection between brands and their consumers. By actively engaging with user-generated content, brands can demonstrate their willingness to listen to and value their customers' feedback. This engagement fosters a sense of community and belonging among consumers, strengthening their loyalty to the brand.

What are the benefits of becoming a UGC creator?

Individuals who choose to pursue a career as UGC creators can reap a multitude of benefits, including:

1. **Creative Expression and Flexibility:** UGC creation provides an outlet for individuals to express their

1

creativity and share their unique perspectives with the world. This flexibility allows creators to explore various content formats and styles, catering to their interests and expertise.

2. **Personal Brand Building:** As UGC creators gain recognition and engagement, they can establish themselves as experts or influencers in their niche. This personal brand building can lead to lucrative opportunities, such as brand collaborations, sponsorships, and even full-time career paths.

3. **Financial Rewards:** UGC creators can monetize their content through various methods, such as affiliate marketing, sponsored posts, and creating their products or services. As their audience grows, their earning potential also increases.

4. **Community Engagement and Networking:** UGC creators often engage with a community of like-minded individuals, both fellow creators and their audience. These connections can lead to valuable collaborations, friendships, and opportunities for professional growth.

How to get started as a UGC creator

Embarking on a journey as a UGC creator involves several crucial steps:

1. **Identify Your Niche:** Passion and expertise are key to success in UGC creation. Choosing a niche that aligns with your interests and knowledge will allow you to produce authentic and engaging content that resonates with your audience.

2. **Select Your Platform:** Different UGC platforms cater to different content formats and audiences. Choose the platform that best suits your niche and content style, whether it's Instagram, TikTok, YouTube, or a specialized platform like Patreon.

3. **Establish Your Brand Identity:** Create a consistent and recognizable brand identity for your UGC profile. This

includes using high-quality images, a compelling bio, and a consistent tone of voice.

4. **Develop a Content Strategy:** Plan your content creation process by developing a content calendar and outlining your ideas. Experiment with different formats and styles to keep your audience engaged.

5. **Engage with Your Audience:** Actively interact with your audience by responding to comments, participating in discussions, and hosting interactive events. Building a strong community is essential for long-term success.

6. **Analyze and Adapt:** Regularly evaluate your content's performance using analytics tools. Identify what resonates with your audience and adapt your strategy accordingly.

7. **Collaborate and Network:** Connect with other UGC creators in your niche to share ideas, collaborate on projects, and expand your reach.

8. **Monetize Your Content:** Explore various monetization methods, such as affiliate marketing, sponsored posts, or creating your products or services. Diversify your income streams to ensure sustainable growth.

9. **Stay Consistent and Patient:** Building a successful UGC career requires dedication and patience. Consistent content creation and engagement are key to attracting and retaining a loyal audience.

10. **Enjoy the Process:** Embrace the creativity and joy of content creation. Find fulfillment in sharing your passions and connecting with your audience.

Chapter 2: Selecting Your UGC Platform

In the dynamic world of user-generated content (UGC), selecting the right platform is crucial for your success. The platform you choose will determine your audience, the type of content you can create, and the overall reach of your UGC endeavors. Let's delve into the diverse landscape of UGC platforms and explore how to make an informed decision.

Popular UGC Platforms

The digital arena offers a plethora of UGC platforms, each with its unique strengths, audience demographics, and content formats. Here's a glimpse into some of the most popular options:

1. **YouTube:** With over 2 billion active users, YouTube is the undisputed king of video content. It's an ideal platform for creators who specialize in vlogs, tutorials, product reviews, and entertaining videos.
2. **Instagram:** Instagram, with its visually driven format, is a haven for photographers, artists, and fashion enthusiasts. Its Stories and Reels features provide ample opportunities for engaging content creation.
3. **TikTok:** TikTok's short-form, trending video format has captured the attention of Gen Z and millennials alike. It's a great platform for showcasing creativity, humor, and dance moves.
4. **Twitter:** Twitter's microblogging format makes it ideal for sharing news, opinions, and quick thoughts. It's a platform where UGC creators can engage in conversations and build a following.
5. **Reddit:** Reddit, with its diverse communities and forums, is a hub for niche discussions and user-generated content. It's a great platform for creators to share expertise and connect with like-minded individuals.

Choosing the Right Platform for Your Niche

The key to selecting the right UGC platform lies in understanding your niche and target audience. Consider the following factors when making your decision:

1. **Audience Demographics:** Identify the age group, interests, and online behavior of your target audience. Choose a platform that aligns with their preferences and habits.

4

2. **Content Format:** Assess the type of content you want to create. If you specialize in videos, YouTube is a natural choice. If you're a photographer, Instagram is a better fit.
3. **Platform Strengths:** Each platform has its unique strengths. Leverage the platform's features to showcase your content effectively. For instance, use YouTube's long-form videos for in-depth tutorials or Instagram's Stories for real-time updates.

How to Set Up Your UGC Profile

Once you've chosen your platform, it's time to create a compelling profile that represents your brand. Here are some essential steps:

1. **Choose a Username:** Your username should be memorable, relevant to your niche, and easy to type.
2. **Optimize Your Bio:** Craft a concise and engaging bio that highlights your expertise and interests. Include links to your website or other social media profiles.
3. **Create High-Quality Profile Picture and Cover Photo:** Use high-resolution, professional-looking images that represent your brand and personality.
4. **Complete Your Profile Information:** Provide all relevant information, such as your location, contact details, and any relevant links.
5. **Start Creating and Sharing Content:** Begin producing and sharing engaging content that resonates with your target audience.

Remember, your UGC profile is your digital storefront. Make sure it's visually appealing, informative, and consistent with your brand identity.

In conclusion, selecting the right UGC platform and setting up a strong profile are crucial steps in your UGC journey. By aligning your platform choice with your niche, audience, and content format, you'll set yourself up for success.

Remember, consistency, creativity, and engagement are the cornerstones of thriving UGC creation.

Chapter 3: Developing Your UGC Strategy

In the ever-evolving landscape of user-generated content (UGC), a well-defined strategy is the cornerstone of success. A UGC strategy outlines your approach to creating, curating, and leveraging UGC to achieve your marketing goals. It's a roadmap that guides your content creation efforts, ensuring that your UGC aligns with your brand identity and resonates with your target audience.

What is a UGC Strategy?

A UGC strategy is a comprehensive plan that outlines how you will utilize user-generated content to achieve your brand objectives. It encompasses various aspects, including:

- **Defining your UGC goals:** What do you aim to achieve with your UGC? Are you seeking to increase brand awareness, drive website traffic, or boost sales? Clearly defined goals will guide your content creation and measurement efforts.
- **Identifying your target audience:** Understanding your audience's demographics, interests, and online behavior is crucial for tailoring your UGC to their preferences.
- **Choosing the right UGC platforms:** Selecting the platforms that align with your niche, content format, and target audience is essential for reaching the right people.
- **Establishing guidelines and expectations:** Set clear guidelines for UGC creation, addressing issues such as content quality, brand consistency, and usage rights.
- **Curating and showcasing UGC:** Develop a process for identifying, selecting, and highlighting high-quality UGC that aligns with your brand and resonates with your audience.
- **Measuring and analyzing results:** Regularly evaluate the performance of your UGC strategy using analytics tools.Track metrics such as engagement rates,

reach, and conversions to assess your strategy's
effectiveness.

How to Create a UGC Strategy

Crafting a successful UGC strategy requires careful
consideration and planning. Here's a step-by-step guide to
get you started:

1. **Define Your Goals:** Determine the primary objectives
   you aim to achieve with your UGC strategy. Are you
   seeking to increase brand awareness, generate
   leads, or drive sales? Clearly defined goals will provide
   direction for your content creation and
   measurement efforts.
2. **Identify Your Target Audience:** Understand the
   demographics, interests, and online behavior of your
   target audience. This will help you tailor your UGC to
   their preferences and increase the likelihood of
   engagement.
3. **Choose the Right UGC Platforms:** Select the platforms
   that align with your niche, content format, and target
   audience. Consider the strengths and limitations of
   each platform to determine the best fit for your UGC
   strategy.
4. **Establish Guidelines and Expectations:** Set clear
   guidelines for UGC creation, addressing issues such
   as content quality, brand consistency, and usage
   rights. This ensures that user-generated content
   aligns with your brand identity and meets your
   standards.
5. **Develop a Content Calendar:** Plan your UGC creation
   process by outlining ideas, assigning responsibilities,
   and setting deadlines. A content calendar helps
   maintain consistency and ensures a steady stream
   of engaging content.
6. **Curate and Showcase UGC:** Identify and select high-
   quality UGC that resonates with your brand and
   appeals to your target audience. Promote user-

generated content on your website, social media channels, and other relevant platforms.

7. **Measure and Analyze Results:** Regularly evaluate the performance of your UGC strategy using analytics tools. Track metrics such as engagement rates, reach, and conversions to assess your strategy's effectiveness.

8. **Adapt and Refine Your Strategy:** Based on your analytics data, make adjustments to your UGC strategy to optimize results. Experiment with different content formats, platforms, and promotion methods to find what works best for your brand.

Elements of a Successful UGC Strategy

A successful UGC strategy incorporates several key elements that contribute to its effectiveness:

1. **Authenticity and Credibility:** User-generated content is valued for its authenticity and credibility. Encourage genuine expressions from your audience rather than overly promotional or scripted content.

2. **Community Engagement:** Foster a sense of community by actively engaging with your audience. Respond to comments, participate in discussions, and recognize and reward high-quality UGC contributions.

3. **Brand Consistency:** Maintain brand consistency in all user-generated content. Ensure that UGC aligns with your brand identity, messaging, and visual style.

4. **Data-Driven Approach:** Regularly analyze UGC performance using analytics tools. Identify what resonates with your audience and adapt your strategy accordingly.

5. **Collaboration and Partnerships:** Collaborate with influencers and industry experts to expand your reach and generate high-quality UGC.

6. **Legal and Ethical Considerations:** Establish clear guidelines for usage rights, copyright, and privacy protection related to user-generated content.

7. **Long-Term Commitment:** UGC is an ongoing process that requires consistent effort and dedication. Commit to long-term content creation and community engagement to reap the benefits of UGC over time.

By incorporating these elements into your UGC strategy, you can create a powerful tool for building brand awareness, engaging your audience, and achieving your marketing goals. Remember, UGC is a conversation between your brand and your audience

Chapter 4: Creating Quality UGC Content

In the dynamic realm of user-generated content (UGC), creating high-quality material is paramount to success. Engaging and informative UGC captures attention, fosters audience engagement, and elevates your brand's presence in the digital landscape. Let's delve into the art of producing high-quality UGC that resonates with your target audience.

Tips for Creating High-Quality UGC Content

1. **Know Your Audience:** Understanding your audience's interests, preferences, and online behavior is crucial for tailoring your UGC to their liking. Research their demographics, social media habits, and engagement patterns to create content that resonates with their tastes.
2. **Focus on Authenticity:** User-generated content is valued for its authenticity. Avoid overly promotional or scripted content; instead, encourage genuine expressions and opinions from your audience. Let your personality shine through to connect with your audience on a personal level.
3. **Prioritize Quality over Quantity:** While consistency is important, it's not everything. Prioritize producing high-quality UGC over churning out a large volume of mediocre content. Invest time and effort in

creating well-crafted, engaging content that delivers value to your audience.

4. **Embrace Diverse Content Formats:** Experiment with different content formats to cater to diverse audience preferences. Utilize a mix of visuals, text, and audio to create dynamic and engaging content. Consider formats such as videos, infographics, blog posts, interactive quizzes, and polls.

5. **Utilize High-Production Values:** Invest in quality equipment and software to enhance your content's production value. Use good lighting, clear audio, and high-resolution images to create visually appealing and professional-looking UGC.

6. **Maintain Brand Consistency:** Ensure that your UGC aligns with your brand's identity, messaging, and visual style. Use consistent branding elements, such as your logo, color palette, and tone of voice, to maintain brand recognition.

7. **Seek Feedback and Adapt:** Regularly seek feedback from your audience through surveys, comments, and social media interactions. Use this feedback to identify areas for improvement and adapt your UGC strategy accordingly.

8. **Stay Current with Trends:** Keep up with emerging trends and challenges in your niche to create timely and relevant content. Stay informed about popular hashtags, viral trends, and audience preferences to keep your UGC fresh and engaging.

9. **Collaborate with Others:** Partner with influencers, industry experts, or fellow creators to expand your reach and generate fresh perspectives. Collaborations can lead to unique and creative UGC that attracts a wider audience.

10. **Embrace Storytelling:** Tap into the power of storytelling to create emotionally resonant UGC. Share personal anecdotes, relatable experiences, and inspiring stories that connect with your audience on a deeper level.

Different Types of UGC Content

The world of UGC encompasses a diverse range of content formats, each with its unique strengths and appeal. Here's an overview of some popular UGC content types:

1. **Product Reviews and Testimonials:** Share genuine reviews and testimonials about products or services to provide valuable insights to your audience. Use visuals, detailed descriptions, and honest opinions to enhance credibility and engagement.
2. **Tutorials and How-To Guides:** Create informative tutorials and how-to guides that teach your audience valuable skills or provide step-by-step instructions for completing tasks. Use clear explanations, visuals, and demonstrations to enhance understanding.
3. **Unboxing and First Impressions:** Share unboxing videos and first impressions of new products or services to provide your audience with an exclusive glimpse. Include detailed product descriptions, usage demonstrations, and honest opinions.
4. **Visual Content:** Capture attention and convey messages effectively through visually engaging content. Utilize high-quality images, infographics, videos, and GIFs to create visually appealing and shareable UGC.
5. **Interactive Content:** Engage your audience and encourage participation with interactive content formats like quizzes, polls, contests, and live streams. Encourage feedback, reactions, and discussions to foster a sense of community.

Remember, the key to creating effective UGC is to understand your audience, cater to their interests, and deliver value through engaging and informative content.

How to Use Video Editing Tools to Create UGC Content

Video editing tools play a crucial role in crafting high-quality video content for UGC. Here's a step-by-step guide to using video editing tools effectively:

1. **Gather and Organize Footage:** Collect and organize your video footage, ensuring it's in a format compatible with your editing software.
2. **Import Footage and Create a Project:** Import your footage into your chosen editing software and create a new project.
3. **Trim and Arrange Clips:** Trim your video clips to remove unwanted sections and arrange them in a logical sequence to create a cohesive narrative.
4. **Add Transitions and Effects:** Enhance your video with transitions and effects to create visual interest and smooth transitions between clips.
5. **Incorporate Music and Sound Effects:**

Sure, here is Chapter 5: Building Your UGC Portfolio

Chapter 5: Building Your UGC Portfolio

In the competitive realm of user-generated content (UGC), a well-crafted portfolio serves as your digital calling card, showcasing your skills, expertise, and ability to create engaging content. A strong UGC portfolio can attract potential collaborators, secure brand partnerships, and open doors to lucrative opportunities.

Why is a UGC Portfolio Important?

A UGC portfolio serves as a valuable tool for aspiring and experienced UGC creators alike. It offers several key benefits:

1. **Demonstrates Your Skills and Expertise:** A portfolio provides a tangible showcase of your UGC creation skills, highlighting your ability to produce high-quality, engaging content that resonates with your target audience.
2. **Attracts Potential Collaborators:** Brands and agencies seeking UGC creators often rely on portfolios to evaluate potential partners. A strong portfolio can attract collaborations with established brands, expanding your reach and influence.

3. **Secures Brand Partnerships:** Brands seeking authentic and engaging UGC often partner with creators who have a proven track record of success. A portfolio serves as evidence of your ability to deliver results, increasing your chances of securing lucrative partnerships.
4. **Opens Doors to New Opportunities:** A strong UGC portfolio can open doors to new opportunities beyond brand partnerships, such as speaking engagements, guest blogging, and even full-time UGC creation positions.

What to Include in Your UGC Portfolio

Your UGC portfolio should carefully curate your best work, showcasing your versatility, creativity, and ability to adapt to different content formats and platforms. Consider including the following elements:

1. **High-Quality Samples:** Select your best UGC pieces that represent your range of skills and experience. Include a variety of content formats, such as videos, images, infographics, and blog posts.
2. **Case Studies and Testimonials:** Showcase the impact of your UGC collaborations by including case studies that highlight the results you've achieved for brands. Include testimonials from satisfied clients or collaborators.
3. **Metrics and Analytics:** Provide metrics and analytics that demonstrate the engagement and impact of your UGC. This could include metrics such as views, likes, comments, shares, and conversions.
4. **Branding and Consistency:** Maintain consistent branding throughout your portfolio, using your logo, color palette, and tone of voice to create a cohesive and professional presentation.
5. **Contact Information:** Display your contact information, including your email address, website, and social

media handles, to make it easy for potential collaborators to reach you.

Tips for Creating a Strong UGC Portfolio

1. **Quality over Quantity:** Focus on showcasing your best work, even if it's a smaller selection. Prioritize quality over quantity to create a more impactful portfolio.
2. **Tailor Your Portfolio to Your Audience:** Consider the type of brands or collaborators you are targeting and tailor your portfolio to their interests and preferences.
3. **Keep It Updated:** Regularly update your portfolio with your latest and best work to reflect your ongoing growth and development as a UGC creator.
4. **Seek Feedback:** Seek feedback from fellow creators, mentors, or industry professionals to refine your portfolio and highlight its strengths.
5. **Promote Your Portfolio:** Actively promote your portfolio on social media, your website, and relevant online platforms to increase visibility and attract potential collaborators.

Remember, your UGC portfolio is a dynamic representation of your skills and expertise. Invest time and effort in creating a strong portfolio that showcases your unique talent and opens doors to exciting opportunities.

Chapter 6: Reaching Out to Brands

In the world of user-generated content (UGC), establishing successful collaborations with brands can propel your career to new heights. By partnering with brands that align with your niche and audience, you can expand your reach, showcase your creativity, and potentially monetize your UGC skills. This chapter will guide you through the process of identifying and collaborating with brands to achieve your UGC goals.

How to Find Brands to Collaborate With

1. **Identify Your Niche:** Clearly define your niche or area of expertise to narrow down your search for relevant brands. Focus on brands that operate within your niche and resonate with your target audience.
2. **Explore Brand Websites and Social Media:** Visit the websites and social media profiles of brands in your niche to identify their current UGC campaigns, brand ambassadors, and collaboration opportunities.
3. **Network with Fellow Creators:** Connect with other UGC creators in your niche to exchange information about brands they've collaborated with and potential partnership opportunities.
4. **Attend Industry Events:** Participate in industry events, conferences, and workshops to connect with brands and potential collaborators in a face-to-face setting.
5. **Utilize Online Collaboration Platforms:** Explore online platforms that connect UGC creators with brands seeking partnerships, such as Upfluence, HypeAuditor, and Collabstr.

How to Pitch Your UGC Services to Brands

Crafting a compelling pitch is crucial for capturing the attention of potential brand partners. Here's how to effectively pitch your UGC services:

1. **Research the Brand:** Thoroughly research the brand you're pitching to, understanding their target audience, brand values, and current marketing campaigns. Tailor your pitch to align with their specific needs and interests.

2. **Highlight Your Strengths:** Emphasize your unique skills, experience, and audience demographics that make you a valuable partner for the brand. Showcase your

past successes and collaborations to demonstrate your proven track record.

3. **Propose Specific Ideas:** Propose specific UGC ideas that align with the brand's messaging and target audience. Demonstrate your understanding of their brand identity and how your content can enhance their marketing efforts.

4. **Quantify Your Impact:** Provide data and metrics to showcase the potential impact of your UGC. Share insights from previous collaborations or demonstrate your ability to generate engagement and reach.

5. **Create a Compelling Presentation:** Craft a visually appealing and informative presentation that highlights your key points and showcases your best UGC work. Use high-quality images, videos, and data visualizations to make a lasting impression.

Tips for Negotiating Successful UGC Collaborations

1. **Understand Your Worth:** Research industry standards and negotiate a fair rate that reflects your skills, experience, and the value you bring to the collaboration.

2. **Define Clear Terms and Conditions:** Clearly outline the scope of work, deliverables, timelines, compensation, usage rights, and any other relevant terms in a written agreement.

3. **Maintain Open Communication:** Communicate openly and promptly with the brand throughout the collaboration process. Address any concerns or questions promptly to maintain a positive working relationship.

4. **Overdeliver and Exceed Expectations:** Exceed the brand's expectations by delivering high-quality UGC that exceeds their initial expectations. This will strengthen your reputation and increase the likelihood of future collaborations.

5. **Gather Feedback and Adapt:** Seek feedback from the brand on your UGC and adapt your approach for future collaborations. Continuous improvement will enhance your skills and reputation as a UGC creator.

Remember, successful UGC collaborations are built on mutual respect, clear communication, and a commitment to delivering high-quality content that benefits both parties. By following these guidelines, you can establish yourself as a sought-after UGC creator and forge valuable partnerships with brands.
Sure, here is Chapter 7: Monetizing Your UGC Career

Chapter 7: Monetizing Your UGC Career

As a user-generated content (UGC) creator, you have the potential to turn your passion for creating engaging content into a thriving career. With dedication, creativity, and smart monetization strategies, you can transform your UGC skills into a source of income and pursue a fulfilling career in the digital world.

Different Ways to Monetize Your UGC Career

The world of UGC offers a diverse range of monetization opportunities, catering to various content formats, platforms, and audience preferences. Here are some of the most common ways to monetize your UGC career:

1. **Brand Collaborations:** Partner with brands to create sponsored content, product reviews, or social media campaigns. Negotiate fair compensation for your services based on your reach, engagement, and the value you bring to the brand.
2. **Affiliate Marketing:** Promote products or services through affiliate links and earn a commission for each sale generated through your unique affiliate link. Choose products or services that align with your niche and target audience.
3. **Merchandising and Products:** Create and sell your merchandise, such as apparel, accessories, or digital products, featuring your brand or designs. Leverage

your UGC platform to promote your products and reach your audience.

4. **Licensing and Usage Rights:** License your UGC, such as images, videos, or music, to brands, media outlets, or individuals for a fee. Grant permission for the use of your content while maintaining control over its ownership.

5. **Paid Memberships and Subscriptions:** Offer exclusive content, perks, or early access to your UGC through paid memberships or subscriptions on your website or platform. Provide value to your subscribers that justifies the membership fee.

6. **Consulting and Workshops:** Share your expertise and knowledge by offering consulting services or conducting workshops related to UGC creation, social media strategy, or personal branding.

7. **Speaking Engagements:** Share your insights and experiences as a UGC creator at conferences, industry events, or online webinars. Get paid for your speaking engagements and expand your reach.

8. **Content Creation Services:** Offer your content creation services to businesses or individuals who need engaging content for their social media, website, or marketing campaigns.

9. **Crowdfunding and Patronage:** Utilize crowdfunding platforms or Patreon to receive financial support from your audience in exchange for exclusive content, perks, or early access to your work.

10. **Freelancing and Project-Based Work:** Offer your UGC creation skills on freelance platforms or take on project-based work for specific brands or

I'm happy to continue writing for you. Please provide me with a specific topic or prompt, and I will do my best to fulfill your request. If you want me to continue writing about Chapter 7, here is an additional section on how to set your rates for UGC collaborations:

How to Set Your Rates for UGC Collaborations

Determining your rates for UGC collaborations is crucial to ensuring you are compensated fairly for your skills, expertise, and the value you bring to the brand. Here are some factors to consider when setting your rates:

1. **Your Experience and Expertise:** Your experience as a UGC creator and your level of expertise in your niche directly impact your value. As you gain more experience and recognition, your rates can increase accordingly.
2. **Platform and Audience Reach:** The size of your audience, engagement levels, and the reach of your UGC across various platforms influence your ability to generate results for brands. Higher reach and engagement justify higher rates.
3. **Content Format and Complexity:** The complexity and time required to create different content formats, such as high-quality videos, in-depth blog posts, or elaborate product reviews, warrant higher rates.
4. **Brand and Campaign Size:** Collaborating with larger, well-known brands often warrants higher rates due to the potential exposure and impact on your career. Larger campaigns with more deliverables may also command higher fees.
5. **Industry Standards and Market Rates:** Research industry standards and rates for UGC creators in your niche to ensure your rates are competitive and aligned with the value you offer.

Tips for Growing Your UGC Business

To successfully grow your UGC career and establish a thriving business, consider these essential tips:

1. **Niche Down and Define Your Audience:** Clearly define your niche and target audience to attract a loyal following and establish yourself as an expert in your field.
2. **Create High-Quality and Engaging Content:** Consistently produce high-quality, engaging content that

resonates with your audience and provides value to the brands you collaborate with.

3. **Build a Strong Online Presence:** Establish a strong online presence across relevant platforms, including your website, social media profiles, and online communities.

4. **Network and Build Relationships:** Actively network with other UGC creators, brands, and industry professionals to expand your reach and explore potential collaboration opportunities.

5. **Promote Yourself and Your Work:** Promote your UGC and services through various channels, such as social media marketing, influencer platforms, and guest blogging.

6. **Analyze and Adapt Your Strategy:** Regularly analyze your UGC performance, audience engagement, and collaboration outcomes to identify areas for improvement and adapt your strategy accordingly.

7. **Stay Updated with Trends and Technology:** Keep up with emerging trends, platforms, and tools in the UGC space to maintain relevance and adapt to the evolving digital landscape.

8. **Diversify Your Income Streams:** Explore multiple monetization avenues, such as brand collaborations, affiliate marketing, and merchandise sales, to diversify your income streams and reduce reliance on a single source.

9. **Seek Mentorship and Guidance:** Seek mentorship and guidance from experienced UGC creators or industry professionals to gain insights and accelerate your growth.

10. **Maintain Passion and Creativity:** Nurture your passion for creating engaging content and continue to explore new creative avenues to differentiate yourself

Conclusion

In the dynamic realm of user-generated content (UGC), the journey of a successful UGC creator is an ongoing process of creativity, collaboration, and continuous learning. By embracing the power of UGC, individuals can transform their passion for creating engaging content into a fulfilling career, building a brand, and monetizing their skills.

Recap of Key Takeaways

Throughout this comprehensive guide, we have delved into the multifaceted world of UGC, exploring its nuances, strategies, and potential for personal and professional growth. Here's a recap of key takeaways to guide your UGC journey:

1. **Understand the Power of UGC:** Recognize the immense value of UGC as a powerful marketing tool, a catalyst for community engagement, and a driving force behind brand authenticity.
2. **Identify Your Niche and Target Audience:** Clearly define your niche, the area of expertise where your passion and skills lie. Understand your target audience, their demographics, interests, and online behavior.
3. **Select the Right UGC Platforms:** Choose the platforms that align with your niche, content format, and target audience. Consider the strengths and limitations of each platform to optimize your reach and engagement.
4. **Develop a Compelling UGC Strategy:** Craft a well-defined UGC strategy that outlines your goals, target audience, content formats, promotion channels, and measurement methods. Adapt your strategy based on data and audience feedback.
5. **Create High-Quality and Engaging Content:** Prioritize producing high-quality, engaging content that resonates with your audience and aligns with your brand identity. Embrace diverse content formats to cater to different preferences.
6. **Build Your UGC Portfolio:** Curate a strong UGC portfolio showcasing your best work, highlighting your skills, versatility, and ability to deliver impactful results.
7. **Reach Out to Brands:** Actively seek out brands that align with your niche and target audience. Craft compelling pitches that demonstrate your value and potential impact.

8. **Negotiate Successful Collaborations:** Negotiate fair compensation for your UGC services based on your experience, expertise, and the value you bring to the brand. Establish clear terms and conditions in a written agreement.
9. **Monetize Your UGC Career:** Explore various monetization avenues, such as brand collaborations, affiliate marketing, merchandise sales, and consulting services, to diversify your income streams.
10. **Continuous Learning and Adaption:** Stay updated with emerging trends, platforms, and tools in the UGC space. Adapt your content, strategy, and monetization methods to remain relevant and competitive.

Tips for Success as a UGC Creator

As you embark on your UGC journey, remember that success is not a destination but an ongoing process of learning, growth, and adaptability. Here are some additional tips to guide you toward success:

1. **Nurture Your Passion:** Cultivate a genuine passion for creating engaging content. Let your enthusiasm shine through to connect with your audience on a deeper level.
2. **Embrace Authenticity:** Stay true to your authentic voice and personality. Avoid overly promotional or scripted content; instead, encourage genuine expressions and opinions.
3. **Consistency is Key:** Commit to consistent content creation to maintain audience engagement and establish yourself as a reliable source of valuable content.
4. **Seek Feedback and Adapt:** Regularly seek feedback from your audience and collaborators. Use this feedback to improve your content, refine your strategy, and adapt to audience preferences.

5. **Enjoy the Process:** Find joy in the creative process of content creation. Embrace experimentation, learn from your mistakes, and celebrate your successes.
6. **Networking and Community:** Actively engage with the UGC community, connect with fellow creators, and learn from each other's experiences. Build meaningful relationships and collaborate on exciting projects.
7. **Embrace Innovation:** Stay ahead of the curve by exploring emerging trends, platforms, and tools in the UGC space. Innovate with new content formats, storytelling techniques, and engagement strategies.
8. **Resilience and Perseverance:** The journey of a UGC creator is not without its challenges. Embrace resilience, persevere through setbacks, and learn from every experience.
9. **Celebrate Your Achievements:** Recognize and celebrate your milestones, achievements, and positive feedback. Your successes will fuel your motivation and keep you moving forward.
10. **Always Be Learning:** Never stop learning and expanding your knowledge base. Attend workshops, take online courses, and seek mentorship to enhance your skills and stay at the forefront of the UGC industry.

Dear Reader,
Thank you for embarking on this journey into the world of user-generated content (UGC). As you've explored the chapters, you've gained insights into the power of UGC, the strategies for creating engaging content, and the potential for building a successful career in this dynamic field.
I hope this guide has served as a valuable resource, providing you with the knowledge and tools to navigate the UGC landscape with confidence. Whether you're a seasoned creator or a budding enthusiast, remember that UGC is a continuous learning process. Embrace experimentation, adapt to evolving trends, and never stop exploring the creative possibilities that UGC offers.

As you continue your UGC journey, I encourage you to embrace authenticity, connect with your audience, and let your passion for storytelling shine through. Your unique voice and perspective are invaluable assets in the UGC world.

Remember, success in UGC is not just about creating viral content; it's about building genuine connections with your audience, inspiring others, and making a positive impact on the digital landscape.

So, go forth, create with passion, and let your UGC journey be a source of fulfillment, growth, and success.

With gratitude

Jai Cadell ❤️ □

www.ingramcontent.com/pod-product-compliance
Lightning Source LLC
Chambersburg PA
CBHW071021290526
45795CB00005B/1887